To the Nia

Also by Jon Glover

Poetry

The Grass's Time (Northern House)
The Wall and the Candle (Northern House)
Our Photographs (Carcanet)

Editions

Notes for a Survivor
poems by Emmanuel Litvinov (Northern House)
The Penguin Book of First World War Prose
(with Jon Silkin)

Jon Glover

To the Niagara Frontier

POEMS NEW AND SELECTED

CARCANET

Acknowledgements

Some of these poems have appeared in Northern House Pamphlets (*The Grass's Time*, 1970, and *The Wall and the Candle*, 1982). Others have appeared in *Poetry and Audience* (Leeds), *PN Review*, *Snog* (University of Sussex), and *Stand*. Thanks are due to the Editors of these journals. Several groups from *Our Photographs* have been read on 'Poetry Now' (BBC Radio 3) in programmes introduced by Jon Silkin and Michael Schmidt.

First published in 1994 by
Carcanet Press Limited
208-212 Corn Exchange Buildings
Manchester M4 3BQ

A CIP catalogue record for this book
is available from the British Library
ISBN 1 85754 055 7

The publisher acknowledges financial assistance
from the Arts Council of Great Britain

Set in 10pt Palatino by Bryan Williamson, Frome
Printed and bound by SRP Ltd, Exeter

Contents

To Elaine, Abby, Rhiannon and Jerry
and to all the Shavers and Glovers

THE GRASS'S TIME

1817. July 21. Fine hot day; but heavy rain at night. Flies, a few. *Not more than in England. My son John, who has just returned from Pennsylvania, says they are as great torments there as ever. At a friend's house there,* two quarts of flies *were caught in* one window in one day! *I do not believe that there are two quarts on all my premises. But, then, I cause all* wash *and* slops *to be carried forty yards from the house.*

William Cobbett   *A Year's Residence in the United States of America*

Lie together, grin, creep, pant, assemble;
convene the kingdom.

Jon Silkin   *Isaiah's Thread*

Praise us,
for surviving, greedy for our neighbour's love
to the touch precious as bread, the moist
dead sustenance.

Jon Silkin   *Famine*

Lake Road in the Snow

In the snow we are quiet,
walking through farm buildings
to the lake, intruders in this flat land
dreamt by Indians waiting for summer.
•The white, unfenced fields are pierced
by corn-stalks and trees falling
in black spikes around us like broken cages.
The road divides the rough, frozen land,
stops at the lake. Clouds hurry
over this emptiness. The ice
is tense and sharp in the angry sun.
Dark woods snap in the wind.
The snow clings like muscle,
pulling at the dry-stalked plants.
And the lake ripples
with the mute colours of the hunter's shot bird.

Trees on the Shoreline

Straight, white logs
sucked dry as they drift in the heat,
broken planks, whole trees,
mingle with the animals
on the open rock.
The shore is a wound to living things,
its unplanted soil shifts with the water,
each grain of humus
the fading shape of fish or bird,
each particle of rock
too large to give nourishment.

Three Stonebirds

I

Rockface,
my wings.
My air marked
with food
and the other lives
sliding past between
moist roots. Webbed
in the earth,
my path is
threaded with flint colours.
This rock, studded
with leaves,
flows with my flight.
Space of the hawk
niched in the wind.

II

Soft quartz streaked
through me,
trees and farms under
my feet. Mist
and sun slide over
my body and clear off.
In the world above
grass rests,
hiding my form
like down.

III

In this spindle shell
my air is chalk.
I am flightless.
I twist through the sand.
The sun scatters in all
the other directions.

Lancashire Landscape

On the summer moorland, rustling, burned,
your cry, dark, like a cleft in the stone,
stretches to the edge of the valleys
and their shuddering rain.
The turning of the landscape –
seasons of rock, ages of fern, coal,
streams running in grit –
is delicate in its life;
quick to give and take, the smallest thing
leaving its trace: colour, bones, peat,
heather's roots niched in the frost-chiselled stone.
Your voice, with the hunched gulls' screams,
curls through the grass like a shell,
intricate, clutching; the grass's time.

OUR PHOTOGRAPHS

Rather I want to emphasise the multiple sites of representation and the crowd's movement among them, for they suggest that the problem of the assimilation of the other is linked to what we may call, adapting Marx, the reproduction and circulation of mimetic capital.

Stephen Greenblatt   *Marvelous Possessions*

These poems from the sequence *Our Photographs* concern a man who leaves his home on a Scottish island for the United States in the nineteenth century. They also concern the place he sets out from and the people who stay behind. His sense of space and of himself changes. His letters home disturb those who remain to face eviction. Who has gone away?

The speaker, or main character, of each poem is identified at the end of each poem. For convenience, the man who leaves his island is called the 'exile'. From the poem 'Islanders' onwards the word is hardly relevant.

Making Ready

It was as though they fell willingly into place.
Behind barred doors and darkened windows
they sat tending evening fires. A few pulled
half-grown vegetables and carried heavy sacks
to secret shelter. After going about their
business in the hopeless private evening
they set themselves to rest in unconscious reward.
The night was cloudy and there was no moon.
Sleep was easy and expected.

I saw a garden where new weeds thickened
entwining and shading each worthless, forced
luxury. By the end of summer they were everywhere.
Then the first gales tore them down and they
matted themselves over the thin unusable crops.
Grass pricked out its slow return. And all around
the people stood unmoved and still. The place was
awaiting completion. They were so utterly
unimportant they were rooted to the spot.

[The exile]

To Quit

'...and leave for your own good.'

So I did not wait for any bailiff or agent. I wanted not even to admit that much of his dispossession. To fight for this land would put me like a speck of dust on that clean accountant's finger. In whatever Capital he wrote his assurances, I saw with what infinite care he might blow away that small encumbrance. Either he held the land, or me. Such ownership lightly edged me off his charts. I crossed from shore to shore. Then by boat to Oban and then to Dundee. Waiting to embark, I sat and watched the evening mist lick out under the sunshine, softening into the steely mudflats of the Tay. On a tiny rectangle of wood, a man painted a picture of the shore with its farms and fat cattle as though it was a desolate and storm-swept beach. Obliterating the marks of men, his landscape brushed out my love, family, blood. Deep in the ship to Boston I woke to the slap and rush of the water at my ear. The painter's grey, heartless waves followed through every night.

[The exile]

10

Two Passengers

Looking out to sea, standing
on deck by the Captain's cabin,
you are firm but at ease.
A regular passenger.

Face immobile, but I feel
you relish this time-
tabled space between
responsible worlds.

Your landscapes! Your flowers!
Taking always the wider view
you blink in the sun, relaxing,
composing the worth of it all.

Meanwhile, the ferry steams
and shudders by the quayside.
My four hundredth crossing
this year; even so, I must

examine the chart each time
and check every gauge. At
four this morning I inspected
the coal yards. Monday:

the Company's crew are
obedient and neat,
fresh from Church
(and the benefits of

Sunday's adult education
classes). We welcome
the passengers with
loyal respect. Despite

our skills in navigation and
engineering they know their
place. I only record one poor
soul removing from the island

today. He will be kept out of
sight until the others have left
the ship. Below decks, for the first
time he smells the machinery of state.

[The ferry boat captain]

Conversation Piece

The Captain had one heavy leather suitcase
that stayed permanently on the ship:
a collection that he added to less and
less frequently now that his voyages
were never (intentionally) more than
forty miles each way. Only at the
half-way point between the two quays
(thirty more minutes) would he sometimes
open the case, having locked his door
and given strict instructions to the
First Officer. Occasionally, he would
choose one object to stand on the table
when a respected client of the Company
was invited to his cabin to pass the time
over an appropriate drink. Today, thinking
of the rich passenger still standing at
the rail, he opened the case and chose
a dried, curled armadillo (from Florida),
a Chinese opium pipe, (his Uncle's)
sketch pad from the Nile delta and
a glass-topped box containing five
mounted scorpions. The ship heeled in a
tide race. He shifted his balance, glanced
at the sky, replaced three of the objects
in the case and slid it under his bunk.
He arranged glasses and a decanter and
opened the door. He spoke to the passenger
who entered briskly, accustomed to being
noticed. They sat opposite each other
at the brass-edged table. Land soon filled
the porthole's view. Five minutes remained
to repossess the savage outer world
in polite, deliberate conversation.

[The ferry boat captain]

The Artist's Grim Humour

'Recorded it.' Not the grass of cattle,
but His. The landscape achieved
for the classics – legend and nobility –
but not for bright Italian saints.
Such coloured morality seems cheap
beside what I know of His wrath.
I have enough to contend with.

I study what etchings come from London.
The copying will teach me though it spoils my eyes.
Their vision, the masters', must have been gifted.
I've not that, it seems, but I'm not content
with my style. Accuracy I can work on.
And when I paint it in with colours
the masters might use I have some escape
from the Church and the muck of my neighbour's farm.
The moving sea parades what anger I can allow.
Secretly, with my finest nib, I might copy
their human figures. Style, style will come,
may come. For now, this formal, public storm
will do. Scrub out the blobbed people. Varnish it.

[The Dundee painter]

The Painter and Science

My paintings assemble in one bright room
their gloomy imprecisions
and accumulate their insults and accusations
leaving so much untouched, unnamed.
Next to the pile I keep an old sextant;
my grandfather was a sea captain.
Its brass is still polished and each
moving lens and filter holds some dignity
in its smooth passage. Tantalizing
and strangely coloured, its sense of place
is immaculate. What might science know!
The sun reflected and turned through
there and there, fixed in metal rings
and green glass; the horizon numbered
by the finest engraving. I know the
thing lies complete, though I cannot use it,
and still I regard guiltily its way
of seeing. In its smooth, teak box
it seems content with the world's spinning
while my poised waves and sunless, unexplored
pastures are mere imagination, simply human.

[The Dundee painter]

On the Ship: Memories

Above the village, the walled graves.
To go up to that ceremony,
climbing into silence,
was no division. That mile stamped
a god's dream over the land.
Our hill held in each stone mark
the words we left between peat and root.

'Worship the house with its boned roof.
Worship the tree with its seasonal berries.
Worship the water, fingering from the hillside.
Stay, stay in every step of grass.
The wind blows sand out of the sea
into this land.'

We once saw another ship pass miles away.
And though there was no way to speak
we all watched it move. Our new freedom
ached without words. I searched the sea
for whales, porpoises, any living thing
that would say the whole sea was not mine.
But there was nothing to know.
The ship held us like a cage,
and salt cracked our skin
till we were disgusted with love.

[The exile]

Islanders

I want to begin that I don't know
how to speak to you.
But that's not true. I have
to say where I am – see:
a salt spring, a creek, a sandy forest.
The water is bitter
and lies in a burned-out log.
I followed an Indian path here
from where I was thrown off the railroad.
I could see the farmsteads. I've learned
not to go there. Children watch
me though, and all the others.
The young see us travelling; their parents
forget such journeys. I go on
to these meeting places and
here are men from the Isles.
And from the islands of Sweden,
Iceland, Finland, fishermen too.
I trap gulls for them.
And why should I stop like these farmers?
Through the trees, I saw a lake
that seemed endless. That's enough.
I don't want their English names.
As they turn their backs on the passing trains
I seem to hurt them, and, perhaps,
they still hurt me. As I drink,
an Indian looks at me and through me
straight at the earth. He was born
near the spring, he says, and he touches
the water for me. I can go now.
You understand this, don't you?
He will take this letter for you all
to some village here. He touches the trees
for each word: Westmannaeyjar, Rauma,
Calgary, Oland. I don't want
to hear the English, or to know their names.

[The exile]

17

Pure

I picked handfuls of fruit. At the edge of the fields, shaded
by sumac and maple, English apples and cherries dropped,
thin and sticky, into the brown stubble. No trace of what-
ever farmstead had once been here with its precious, sweet
fruit; the seeds, carried from some old, careful orchard;
saplings guarded in this heat and the dispiriting ice. A new
field edges into the forest here, and the trees, too, uproot
the first paths, fences and corner posts. But deeper, by the
creek, the Indian's well stands in its log.

> And again I peered into the log.
> The water was smoothed by the
> wood's fiery colours: copper
> and salt sifted their warmth
> through the clouds' reflections.
> The new world, its freshness,
> its spiked, dangerous brilliance,
> softened into a depth
> I dared not measure.
>
> Deft mosses, elegant spiders
> spangled each nearby tree.
> But not the smooth well.
> Alone and silent, away
> from the wasps, it marked
> its own territory; its human
> purposes a permanence of sorts.
> Pure? Or pure indifference?
> I can't see my face in it.

[The exile]

Away

Pool of water, pool of water. I have thrown three stones now and you tell me nothing. I want some voice, some speech from this place. But my stones fall in the dull weed and will not match my anger. The letter comes from the other place and talks of endless forests and the long wait by the railroad tracks. Where is he? I have come to the shore perhaps to see where that world might be. In the village they watch me. I am now in the outside. Rocks, rocks, are these the same sounds he hears? He writes much of the heat, his gun, the moving bands of people. No place for birth, marriage, death. Nowhere that is the outside, the far. He travels day by day and yet seems to possess it all. I have left the village with his letter. Outside by the rock pools I am outside, in silence, and I possess nothing.

[A villager, the second exile]

Harvest

Split from the rock,
their yellows and blacks smear to green;
the mussels' soft shine lies bruising in the sun.
Such stillness seems not to have needed life.

Yet they patch together their sharp, stitched colony
against whatever element frets the stone.
Each clasps a portion of the sea that aches
over it, lapping its primitive fresh gape.

For a time there is flesh: liquid, defiant,
unhurt even by the stupid, tiny pearls
that crush out to dust,
without sound, in the sand.

Their shape is savage,
bound to the rock,
small, black, sacred books
opening and closing for their own commemoration.

Over the machair, I see those incessant, pulling mouths,
twenty sheep still on the eyebright and thyme.

[A dispossessed villager]

The Dream

Fear? The morning wind ruffled into my sleep.
Through one eye I saw a praying mantis
jerk to stillness on my arm. God! the cold
sunshine made the thing flame against the sky.
When the last of my breath had left me
I jumped from shelter casting the harmless insect
away and I dared not look at my arm
till the air grew hot and I stopped to rest.
On my skin that spring of life and death
shivered all day. When I closed my eyes
I remembered the dream: I stood beside a
child's small grave in a sandy forest.
In the dream I slept nearby when the
mourners were gone. And, waking then,
the insect's light feet pinned death in
my limbs and I had to kick out and run from it.
I ask you now, who has died?

[The exile]

Letters and Fictions

One in America, the rest now scattered
or dying here by the shore, the recovery of love
seems beyond any task permitted by hunger and cold.
God knows, I believed no one could just go.
The world was not to be trifled with.
I was a tenant and obedient to the will of the place.
Though still I thought my love crossed enough boundaries.
And now his journeys consume my present,
and his past is freed, cancelled rather,
by each new marvel. He describes flowers in such
     profusion
I think he is mad. Paradise? It wasn't promised
for the price of a voyage. The sea and the land are work,
work and death, and as for love
all I want is to finish it and sleep.

'I saw enormous lilies. They were red and gold.
The summer sun is so bright I could not believe
nature could go on matching it, radiance for radiance.
Orchards, wheat-fields and the rich, cracking mud.
The smell of heat. Who needs to praise God
amongst this opulence? I met a painter who simply
records what is there: orchids, poison ivy and
the humming-birds no Northerner has seen.
This observation, again and again, is love.
My senses grow, and desire.'

Now the village is burnt, his letters will have no answer.
They become fictions.

                    [A woman reads the exile's letter]

22

Nature

I stop for hours to watch butterflies. I am tempted not
to draw them but to collect them. Sometimes I think
I would like to watch them grow and breed. Then I
fancy arranging them, to kill and preserve their
abundance, their colours, their alien delicacy. Still
I have nowhere for this. And, finally, to set things in a
house would create a stillness shut from the sun, a
civilization that I go on trying to leave.

From earth colours and its skin
of thin, dry crystal,
its fragile liquids snap out and are gone.
Without tenderness
or anything sensual
it holds my gaze, meets food,
flower or parasite
across void after void:
the blank spaces come
and go on coming.

Touching their fine dusts
tempts me to indifference –
all those designs, fantastic eyes,
and mimicked leaves grow
without fear or knowledge,
display purpose and beauty
without love and die raggedly
or freeze. These human qualities
want them collected, row upon row,
preserving each as a separate
kingdom of man's desire?
Like cold, pinned galaxies?

[The exile]

Treasures

The faint smell of a distant, injured skunk
announced the evening's parley. The sky cleared
from orange to green to blue to perfect
black, thrilling with stars. Horizons faded.

I was alone with the closed, ravenous
freedoms where bats swung their zany forage
trails through the trees in the rich air that was
still and dry and sweet. Insects' noisy, rattling

talk, the small animals' feverish hunt
and owls' insistent, proud flight settled in
their routines. Sightless yearnings apportioned
night's energies, consumed day's peaceful

heat. Sitting beside the road, I heard a
desperate scuffling in a nearby ditch.
When it had stopped, I felt in my pocket
for the brilliant monarch wings and goldfinch

feathers picked from the roadside's coarse litter
that morning and lovingly wrapped in clean
paper. I dropped them into the reeds. When
I woke, at dawn, a contorted, blinded

snake lay by the ditch. It discounted all
innocent concern as its lurid blood
dried; dismal treasure, night's discovery.
Unsure, daylight cajoled its gritty wound.

[The exile]

24

Portraits and Love

Remembering, trying to love, I write about standing by
the shore, I want your face, not fixed as in a portrait but
moving. And automatically you turn away. Why should
this come so naturally, to make you go back over the
sand? Trees, the valley, herons flap slowly over the bay.
Gone. The picture smirks in the sun: the past unloved, its
imagined objects dispossessed.

> The sand pushes its colours
> into the sun: streaks of silver,
> lavender spines of seaweed,
> green and rock-black wood, the drift
> and smell of the sea and all
> that the other continents spit.
> There are close-nailed crates,
> their bright fruit wrung out;
> nets; rust; a tube of ointment
> labelled in Russian script;
> and pumice, floating cargo
> of a battered ship: stone flung
> and floated absurdly, suds
> of the earth's heat,
> on to this cooler shore.

So nothing: waste, nicely composed. Your anger is there,
without question and I don't care.

[The exile]

The Wall and the Candle

The stone wall (ridiculous to speak
of its loved creation) weighs out
a hillside field. Community of man
and frost-split rock? moss and insect?

So much rough work; and the bracken will rise
each summer to hide it, rain slides
through it: such warnings are some
recompense. Boundaries marked naturally

but to order, and thus instructive,
they apportion life or landscape
as you will. In composed degradation
the tame and the wild meet at this

closed corner: earth floor, turf
and the one wall which runs back
for miles, blackly counting its
larger property. And the light

permits less and less of the world
to serve our winter. My candle flaps
its huddled ceremony of power over
beasts; drips away. Spray, frost, dew,

and the first shoots of the walled crops
glitter nearby. But hypnotically,
in the dark, the tallow trickles and clouds
to a cluster of smoky jewels

as the flame, someone's commodity,
reaches the end of what is paid for.
The night and the wall insist we have just
such molten value in your rich imagination.

[A dispossessed villager]

Seen from a Distance

The sea is glassy today. Appropriately, a well-polished steam launch brings the tropical garden expert to rig out the most sheltered hillside in flowers of the uncultivated world. Botany for pleasure (and proof that the climate isn't so bad). And, indeed, we must be up to date, experimental even, in retirement.

Directing the erasure of the native wood the gardener plans a complex wilderness. Sitting beside his case of neatly labelled seeds he displays prints of Indian hill-stations and African jungle. Later, in the house, the owner tours his water-colours of Scottish castles deep in New England forest and Malayan plantations. Eucalyptus and palm, gathered in such savage places, take quickly and bring the Empire together.

> From the cliff-top the sea's
> drift and grain spreads perfectly
> beneath the hot, rising air.
> Quickly trying the sun, its
> black, slithering communities
> circle, stiffen and vanish
> under the brittle light.
> Over on the shadowed side
> of the bay one fisherman,
> darkly clothed, lets his boat
> drift and leans nearer and
> nearer the bleak surface.
> Slowly, the wash of a steamer
> bends the whole thing.
> The boat slops upright.
> Light settles again,
> allowing nothing to be seen.

[The landlord]

The Last Funeral: Maps and Images

'Compared to [Staffa] what are the cathedrals or the
palaces built by men!'
Sir Joseph Banks, James Cook's naturalist, 1772

A long tide hunked the rolling, abraded flesh
up the sand. Cornered and shredded in its
devoted rock pool its translucent pall
trickled away to the low, Spring surf. Briefly
to be discovered; an odd gesture of creation;
a stammer on the landscape's tongue,
ah! demanding the distinct language of Nature.

Six hours distant clamour and the sea
dutifully replaced its simple map over the bay.
The rock pool and its contents were erased;
the matter withdrawn, unsightly and unsited.
A tide race, beyond the point, proffered its own
careful solution; the true contours softly
dismembered; breathless, shining liquids;

incomparable, another record to be unspoken. And so,
as though wonderfully invisible, their cathedrals –

[The landlord]

Remembering the History Book

The Romans: clear line drawings on stiff, glazed paper.
A neat river curves in imperturbable perspective
beside a spaced and fearless wood. A horizon, gentle
hills; the sky's intense blue conveyed by parallel lines
ruled in a clever expansion. Three birds, the sun, two
  clouds.
Four slaves tend the gardens, tie up a boat, bring wine
to the mistress who sits politely beside a mosaic
in the centre of her villa. (The mosaic is preserved,
we are told, though its colours are disappointing.
Better in the line drawing? Well, more quickly passed
  over.)
There is a detail: a snake, a bird singing, two dogs
strain from the patterned edge towards a delicate
  fountain.
Its clarity, its divided loyalties are there to walk on.

          Your breath, your heart-beat
          is laid out in stone. The quick
          feathers, the weight of your
          eyes: a colonial arrangement.
          Progressive, civilized,
          its persistence relishes
          the living. Consuming songs
          flatly hymn the dangerous
          master. Wonders, aqueducts,
          columns of words, prescribed
          cruelties; these, our foundations.
          Our eloquent wars engrave our
          possessions. Industry thrives.

                              [The exile]

Another History Book

Sixteenth century engravings
review the conduct of the native
inhabitants. Imagine the artist
beginning his official duty
with the quickly sketched first
sight of the coastline, first
forest, first Indians. Then
the brutal rites and wars.
Here, the classical mode is
strongest. His humanistic
training matures as he attends
to the bodies carefully dis-
membered for burning and scalps
held over a fire for smoky
preservation. Torture, medicine,
retribution learned from which
gods? Shaking and sick in his
cabin he unwraps his precious
paper and prepares a fitting
record. It is all clarified,
(but did he see that?) as
he sweats out his vision of
perfect proportion. The Italian
anatomists will not free his
eyes. The more he sickens and
the more he disbelieves the
greater his technical assurance.
His explorations bravely continue
with turtles, snakes and alligators.
On returning to London
he finds that he has dropped
completely out of fashion.

[The exile]

New Maps: Exchanging Gifts

Passing the boundaries of the early maps,
the partitions of major rivers, coastlines,
hills and lakes we continue a conquest,
in outline, at least. A picture story
of what has been walked across and seen.
The remaining possibilities are disproportionately
small (on paper). Far into the interior, by the
high falls, comes a point of exchange. The price
of further discoveries is high: all that historic
vision, truth for truth. But the unmarked land
demands its revelation. Accounts must be rendered.
Each gives the other the articulate sense of where
he is. The passing of gifts begins a new record
which settles its view like ink on a printer's
stone. It will be reproduced and sold.

[The exile]

Wasted Talent

And now, painting the town, I seem to have
still more choice views. I set up my easel
in a field from where I can see the whole
thing: after the wheat and poppies
the first houses, mills and chimneys,
spaces where roads and rivers flow,
the railway's cutting towards the
domed town hall. Bricks and slate
deliver blocks of mass, weighty colours,
after the modern fashion. On the road
to my left a farmer walks into town,
three mill workers walk to their
cottages. They pass beside an elm
and a dusty barn. Putting in all that
detail gives movement and a hidden
story. So what is this town
(a piled, squared-off echo of
tall clouds) surrounded by flowers,
hedges and my representative figures?

I set up again in a lane behind a high mill.
My stool and easel scrape on the cobbles
as I shift to look closer at the moss,
the sky reflected in a large puddle,
the weeds enlivening a disused chimney pot.

I painted one brick, bright and wet as a
ruby sea-anemone, its perspective
studiously correct. A triumph.

[The Dundee painter]

32

Time Out

Taking a journey to the West Coast I left industry behind and sat expectantly in the train for a first sight of a new sea, its highly reputed light and its Romantic islands. And there . . . At a halt before the last descent to the coast I jumped down and pulled my luggage and painting things out too. Leaving the cases with a signalman I walked past the platform to the edge of a steep incline. I started work immediately. The coast curved in towards a placid harbour sheltered by small, low islands, and in the distance, slightly misty, but luminous and expectant, the first Hebridean mountains. A backcloth of theatrical splendour! A clue, a dream, a temptation!

But how to confine the stone,
quayside warehouses? The stacked
fish crates? Arranged on the
pier for their necessary journeys
oil drums, tea chests and fire
wood, and, between the end
of the railway line and the
steam-ship berth the rounded
stocks of coal. Those natural
resources, graded and respected
concluded this holiday composition;
a landscape not quite good
enough: unmarketable again.

[The Dundee painter]

Our Photographs

'If cows clatter to the iron-stained stream.
If the weight of a stone displays man's work.
If the summer's hot mud puffs up into a mist of flies.'

Remember our qualities recorded
in proper fabrics that weave
through the photographic paper.
We were still, attentive,
and watched the eyes, fears,
the other people's looks of how it was
that light out here in salt and silver.
Portraits: a thorough chemical process,
like visiting the lawyer for a deed,
a will, confirming ownership.

This, a house, and a road going west.
Trees around the edge are not there
part of the meaning. It's a road
that goes somewhere and that's important.
But light smudges over the windows
and the horizon is black despite the sun.
All that's left is what you don't want
to see. The picture won't care for you.
What we composed and framed, beyond death,
is your worthless trash, like history.

[The exile]

The Antique Shop

Pillowed, sickly surfaces;
established fabrics; covetous
gloss; brass-edged, approved
memories; the scored, wooden
weights of age; the limpid
scars of work, of prized
utility, of love aching in
the shiny dark (family ties
iridescent in a newly silvered
mirror). Breathless, the blank
spots crowd the Victorian
looking-glasses which top
the soft drawers of miniatures,
unlocked cases of gold and jet,
dull, crimped lockets:
the catches' pretty betrayal –
final, unloved objects of love,
cloudy, unreflective and public.
Each practised hinge swings
wide the disproved values, loosing
the unnamed faces of the dead, briefly
fingered by the future auctioneers.

[The exile]

35

Meal Times

For Susanna Patterson

Musical clock: symphonies of bird-song, built
'with the best materials and up to date factory
methods'. Reeds and pipes twitter their marvels
across the polished table, surprise the upholstery,
open all doors. Inside its case, the wood is razored
clean. Outside, pictured, aged with a penknife,
it pronounces a wild authenticity. Methodical
springs untwist into sound that glitters between
the knives and hisses in the glasses (each
with its bulging, reflected window frames.
Catching the sun!) Wound, observed and dusted,
it times the maple sugar, the gales, the silver's
tarnish. It allows for work with a natural note.
Such democratic joy outclasses the old continent.

[The exile]

Commercial Art

Although, in this painting, the North Sea
is a true, whistling grey; although the clouds
race with unsettling clarity; although
the measured, spiky whitecaps crease and spray
the chosen breadth of water as far
as the eye can see this clipper tips the waves
with inexcusable weightlessness (at an angle
as bravely jaunty as that struck by the pre-
Muybridge race-horse in the next canvas
whose two front legs reach forward and
back legs trail, as though trapped,
while it prices up the aristocratic turf).

The artist has added a few spots of colour
(triumphant sunshine between the worst,
most bulbous clouds, for example, and a
bright ensign and pennant) which assure
the Line's trim future, running before
the wind, confident of the Trades. And,
a nice detail, the Master's dog stands
to attention (though the likely crates of
chickens and harassed sheep seem invisible)
beside the wheel, singled for the Company's
honour even if implausibly balanced.
Passing by this lucky rigging we see

'Hazy Cornfield', 'Lakeside Pebbles', 'Two
Children in a Tree', 'The (forgotten) Shoe'.
Neatly glazed, commerce, adventure and
moving landscapes outrun their times.
The walls invite decoration but the occasions
just escape, outgrowing their trophies,
nudging from behind the entrancing scrap.

[The exile]

The Landlord's Northern Summer

The holly tree shines
and flickers its pale,
summer leaves. A flock
of sparrows dares its
cool, unreliable caves
for the season's grubs
and tumbles out into
the brittle light.
Then tries the crude,
tattered roses that
thud on the window,
careening the new stems
that bend, scratch and
grieve against the wall
to press home their
flowering. The wet ground
unseals its final larvae,
and drifts of midges
curdle the sudden air.
Swifts bestride these
clouds of proven luxury.

The landlord, alarmed, sealed this document, queried two words in the Dictionary and was certain, after consulting the Field Guide, that one of the sparrows was a goldfinch. Then, while boiling water for his coffee, he refined the memory of a lizard that he had seen slowly traversing a warm house wall just below the eaves late, one holiday night in the South. There it was, lazily gripping the cracked plaster, curving radiantly over the surplus heat. Certain, he toppled a forest, cleared the lakeside and, firmly, in the beds of shale, plotted a power station.

[A more recent landlord]

Defining the Past

The afternoon was hot and misty. The lake was flat
and yellow. Thirty children and a teacher walked
in silence to the end of the road and then scrambled
down the steep bank to the narrow shoreline.
High clouds bloomed in the mist. The light became
greyer. The children gathered round the teacher
as he stood proudly against the bank: a lesson
in geology. They looked down at the slatey rock on
which they stood and noted the angle at which it
sloped into the water, split by parallel fissures
and decaying into powdery shingle. Above that, the
edge of brown, sandy soil, six feet of glacial
wash-out, old rivers and silty floods. Here, an inch
of dark red grit: imagine that clearly coloured
layer rolling off for miles three feet under farms
and forests. The sky was divided now by a hard edge,
the taunting sunlight's frill narrowed as green
and purple shreds brushed the tree tops. At the top
of the bank a few inches of dark loam plumed with
grass and silver, oozing roots: nature's latest
achievement. But the children were no longer looking
at the strata of the place's million year history.
The lightning cracked and they ran, broke into
thunderous freedom, the torrents drumming in their
     heads.
They kicked and slithered up the bank, across a field
and towards a wood. Dangerously splashing from tree to
tree and sucking the water that ran down their faces
they pushed through a hedge on to a farm track and
reached a barn where they sheltered beside calm horses.
They crouched breathlessly on the dusty floor.
The teacher caught up with them and turned their escape
to good account. The barn's construction and timbers
were of great historical interest. For tomorrow
he planned an interesting lesson on static electricity.

[The exile; now a teacher?]

39

Evening in the Museum

Filtered sunshine sweetens the glass,
hollows the shades of velvety display
and picks out the day's new dust.

In the evolutionary sequence,
this polished room honours the suave,
tongueless shells –

the uncashable, spell-binding
legacies of which ancestors?
And then the curtained, air-

proof cases of Victorian exotic
moths, ranked in odourless, worthy
burial. Is it so important

that the life has gone? Classified,
interchangeable conquests enrich
the collection. Each pink or yellow

twisting periwinkle as mathematically
courteous and out of reach as its Latin
tag (Littorina Littorea). Bones,

artifacts, dead languages: the quaint
defences and plaguey, quarantined jokes
of the old days. The guards lock up.
Safely, the museum collects itself.

[The exile?]

Rumours of War in the East

On the front page the advertisements for
newly staked land. Details of soil, water,
drainage and the newest roads. On page two
births and marriages and deaths, drawings
of winter's storm damage to property,
and a bridge swept down the creek
in March floods, floating 'like a dismasted
tea clipper' in the lake. An explanation
of a new plough, the appointment of a mayor,
a minister and a station master in the nearest
large town. Page three: Congress, the Indian
question, election addresses. A new wind
band is to play for a dance on mid-summer's
eve. Finally, the weddings of European
princes, an announcement of a new novel
in serial form by Charles Dickens,
Imperial cavalries take up position,
the just set sail to administer the peace.
Lancashire cotton exports continue
to astound the Royal Exchanges.

Here, then, a selection
of important items
for storage or display.
On the wall beside the
sunlit window-frame
the librarian tacks up
a mounted collection
of arrow-heads ploughed
up in the nearby fields
this Spring. On a table
underneath she rests a
careful, copperplate
explanation (written
after consulting the
school teacher). Later,
they are to be lent to
the County Museum.
Pleased by the warm day
she picks daffodils and

arranges them next to
her work of scholarship.
The readers have left.
She folds the newspaper
and drops it into
its proper rack.

[The exile?]

TO THE NIAGARA FRONTIER

*The massacre of the Devil's Hole is often referred to as the first 'strike' in
American history, a strike against the introduction of labor-saving
machinery by the substitution of wheeled vehicles drawn by horses or
oxen for Indian carriers; but it is now generaly conceded that the Senecas
were associated in the Pontiac conspiracy and had arrived at the portage
from their settlements in the Genessee valley just one day too late to have
changed the result at Detroit...In the spring of 1764 Sir William
Johnson came to Fort Niagara with an impressive array of British regu-
lars and colonial troops, and notified the Senecas that he had instructions
to 'wipe out the tribe'.*

J. Boardman Scovell   *A Short History of the Niagara Portage*

*Every sound was hushed by the sense of an unnatural tremor beneath our
feet like the first heave of an earthquake, almost at the same instant the
center of the bastion blew up with a terrific explosion and a jet of flame
mingled with fragments of timber, earth, stone and bodies of men rose to
the height of one or two hundred feet in the air and fell in a shower of ruin
to a great distance all around.*

An eyewitness at Fort Eire, August 1814

*Then, when I felt how near to my Creator I was standing, the first effect,
and the enduring one – instant and lasting – of the tremendous spectacle,
was Peace. Peace of Mind, Tranquility, Calm recollections of the Dead,
Great Thoughts of Eternal Rest and Happiness: nothing of Gloom or
Terror. Niagara was at once stamped upon my heart, an Image of Beauty;
to remain there, changeless and indelible, until its pulses cease to beat, for
ever.*

Charles Dickens   *American Notes*

Thirty Miles East of Niagara

For Dorothy Shaver

I

How could any of us now choose
to survey and claim such a forest?
Mine? Knocking in corner-posts just west
of the termite track and white, flood-cleaned
pebbles must have been a precious, if
practical, after-thought in the holy
work of assaying tracts of redeemable
power: the easy pride in stripped ground
and fire. Flights of smoke signal
a new community at rest and play,
yes, eased into its ideas of possession,
flickering passions stacked against the
retreating territories and made like gifts;
a textual matter, for learning
and working a passage to interpretation.
But the sun, the unseen minders' scampering
feet, the shadows beyond that tree and
that one (click, click) tell, tell tales.

II

Measure it good. The future passes quick;
manifest shocking obligations
against the acres and furlongs; each spade-
cut a new name, demanding subjects
of history and science; allegiances
to make sense of fear. The old inhabitants
freeze dry into wild memories beyond
any electric fence; untouchable,
they are charged with what I came for. Indict
their grave plots, dig the names deep as you can,
wall up and map the worries of our love,
our incisive generation: small plots
of doom, recording, like power stations,
our energy's consumption, our persistent,
crackling guilt. What drew us here is rubbed and

45

stained into the soil like a lost pigment –
there to caress and love as though hotly
begging for forgiveness in the freedom
of our historical society.

III

'Jacob Fitts from Mansfield New Jersey
Articled Land 1809
First Settler 1810
Site of First Log Cabin
Between Ridge Road and the Lake.'

'Humphrey Sharpsteen came to Niagara County in
1815 in search of land. He bought a tract
that extended from the Haight Road south along
the west side of Quaker Road to the line where
later the railroad tracks were built. He married
in 1816 and had a family of nine children.'

'The first school to serve in the Town of Somerset
was a log building that was built about 1½ miles
west of what is now Somerset Corners. Masten
Sherwood was the teacher.'

'David Barker Born Vermont 23-2-1794
Took up land 1815
Wed Vania Herendeen 1820
Built Brick House 1834
Died 1886 Quaker Cemetery.'

'Quaker Cemetery Society of Friends 1824
Denton and Haight gave lands
Stone Wall added 1852 Brick Meeting House-
East torn down after 1900.'

IV

Articled, taken up, built.
On this land the priorities
must have defined themselves:
ownership, food, shelter, learning,
worship and, quite separately,
small cemeteries in the fields;
gifts of land in the land,
their marks and claims
on our memories.

It must have seemed a fair risk,
fertile and flat, easily won,
(blessed even, in retrospect),
and made into bequests in the
simplest terms. So there it was:
identified with other gods, seed
and fodder, horse supplies and ploughs,
blue-prints, money and marriage bonds.

V

European Names, so natural,
become the details of our lovely, safe
environment. Roadside signboards offer
a past for our educated journey
from one community to the next as
we drive down the Haight Road to Quaker Road,
through Barker, past West Somerset's graveyard
to the Town Line Road and past the boundaries
westward. Driving from clearing to clearing
the settlers' names pass by, transferred again
to towns and shops and factories. Their lost
pioneering friendship's paths enable
us to slip so easily through places
of lonely, daily labour, of fear, of
disbelief; and on to the older names.

VI

Along the Ridge and up the great escarpment,
following the Niagara-Mohawk
power lines to their source, we join the other
people being moved to view the Falls. This
new, more crowded society of friends
has chosen to holiday with Nature
not to work it. Bussed along the numbered
observation points we welcome the moment's
guarded risk, and smile at the accepted
clothes and poses of each travelling culture
as couples and families and guided tours
stop for photographs by torrent and rainbow.

VII

We halt each other, gesturing, quickly
apologising, for shot after shot
of our triumphant faces, the falling
water partly hidden, while beneath our
feet the Power Plant works, and, down river, rank
on rank of cable offers a sort of
energy back to the settled people.

But who owns this now? And who chooses these
lessons and ceremonies? What people
haunt the tree-lined gorge? The Parks Commission
trims away the dangerous edges, sells safe
souvenirs, though the spray and thundering
water are real enough. So what do we want
from our hundreds of snaps? From our grateful
faces with all that in the misty background?
Simply to record that for two minutes
we have stood here? To stake our claim on
this natural world, the photographer's split-
second territory?

The camera
returned to my pocket we walk slowly
back to the car, queueing for a drink at
the water fountain with smart Japanese,
French and Irish Girl-Scouts
and curious Amish honeymooners
and smile at each other. Smile in the sun
for our children's sake; for all the helpless
love that isn't in the colour-prints; for
the real dare-devils, far away from here
who may have thought of our peace of mind: their
sweetcorn fields, quiet cattle, perfect peaches.

Cicadas sing and clatter in time through
the open car windows, however far
we go, and however fast, towards home,
chanting their friendship throughout the warm night.

Pleasant Valley

Onondaga, Iroquois – streetnames,
titles to banks and museums: words
from such a recent past preserved
in our forms of writing, our cultured
script. It seems all we've got (all
we've deserved) – a neater prison,
a cheaper zoo, a file of names
adopted like those of the European
immigrants; conquered, the sounds
of ancestors. Displayed on city
towers by machined stone, metal
and neon, a working dictionary
that glosses success in the Empire
State while other languages
reach the dead of winter, their
forgotten season.
               And here, midsummer
in Pleasant Valley, we buy maple
candies and cans of syrup from
the farm fridge at Pumpkin Hollow.
Out of this brash, commercial cold
comes what's left of the Five Nations'
Spring luxury. From the silent snow,
wind-chill and black night sky
the trees tap an irrepressible dream,
reducing, reducing – the whole boiling
forest offering a transforming gift
like the golden ore of bees waiting
for the air to be outspread and free.

Junk Shop

For Elaine

An intimate world of collected,
redundant things; accessories to household
pride and each body's growing pains.
Recurring images that generations
have left as ugly: our parents', our own
childhoods' delights disinfected
and propped between old mirrors and toys.

Well, here we are, revisiting what it was
that slipped from our sight as the desirable
new materials, shapes and fabrics left home
with our dead relatives, our own past years.
A box of scratchy records, shelves of Romance
and religious advice to the newly-wed,
discarded bridal veils, shiny Japanese

salt cellars. Beside the dull, white fridge
and shapeless baby clothes are heaps of
almost-complete years of *National Geographic*'s
happy, '50s empire; in these very clothes
tourists walk from their cars to admire giant
redwoods and caress cameras that accumulate
here with tin-openers and candle-snuffers.

These handy mechanical aids to spry
illumination stiffen on the higher
shelves into an untouched, scareless fixed-
focus. Will the cracked leather bellows
re-fold? Are the shutter speeds fast enough
for our up-to-date film? Might they capture
me? All given to be put again to good

use: for charity, for the poor. We leave,
sentimentally, with what we chose not to choose.

Field Day

It's an easy target: domestic, folksy
and all-inclusive. The crowds are
earnest, familiar and God-fearing
though the rooms filled with children's
crayoned pictures of the 'good pasture'
and paper plates cling-filmed with
chocolate cake and potatoes seem
quickly deserted, even by their prized
families. Yet all are saved;
each exhibit has a ribbon from the
committee and the sponsors. To be entered
is to be good enough. And why not!

Through the barn of caged rabbits
and rare poultry we come to the auction shed:
the end of the show for the shampooed
lambs and brushed heifers. Over one stall
the sign says 'Meet Meat', and another
'Raise a Fork for Pork'. The same local
restaurant buys them in each year
for the freezer – a rich conclusion
to this living Pastoral, the good
shepherd's work grilled to order.

And down the aisle of local organisations –
Drug Awareness; Lingerie Parties; Clean
Water; Taxidermy; Engineering Opportunities
for Women – sit the Vietnam Veterans.
There is no flock near them; behind the table
sit four lean, critical men my age, in dark
clothes, offering a few books and leaflets
in camouflage colours. Is there nothing
wanted from that war? The rest of the day
is still for sale. But their memories?
The Big Wheel, The Tilt-a-Wirl-a,
The Swizzler; close your eyes, hold
your stomach. There's not much to laugh at.

The Restored Canal

For Lowell and Coleen Shaver

Black and green veneers
stop the waters;
layers of reflected trees
and vines; furnished
everglades; velvets
in a polished mirror;
sunlight going nowhere.

Rich splashes of light
that grace no river
but bloom like the best dyes
and pigments of our industry,
man-made, analysed,
and alluring; squeezed
from heavy lead tubes
on to a Victorian palette
and brushed. Imagine
a chemist working
for those variant darks
and the dealer's pride;
limitless depth
on the good canvas
(stretchers, poisons,
oils – the artist's
materials) transports
of delight.

　　　　All this
landscape newly licked
into shape, colours restored,
artifacts glazed for
pleasure. *Towpath, culvert,
lock, aqueduct* – such words
offer their respectful
divisions, the names
for what I see,
like my grandfather's
paintbox: a shining
world of lost labour.

Fairground

Having parked the car, late afternoon,
('Just run your ass backwards in'),
we were deep already amongst the sideshows.
Not the usual shooting ranges and fluffy toys
for a well aimed coin, but the private
exhibitions of what else our genes can do.
To fire and aim and eat and drive a cart
easy round a figure of eight and spin
screaming and crying back to childhood
(though then you didn't dare)
on some electric ride – these,
the acceptable faces of knowledge and
skill. But here, beside the cars, the come-on
is a six-legged goat frisking oddly
with three quite normal lambs. A tape
played on, seductively explaining
the bold, fairground lettering and red
and yellow portraits: the only pig
with a baby's face, the smallest woman,
the cow with two heads. Just pay, step in
to see real freaks (but if they're real
is it still permitted? and if they're not,
what charms and stitching? and why
do we want to be so conned?).
I saw no-one entering the doors
of the trailer; the endless voice
was lost in other music. I rehearsed
such words as 'un-enjoyable', 'grotesque',
and 'tasteless'; redundant commentary,
of course, and walked quickly on in silence
till we reached, relieved, the comic book
trials of strength and mirrors and haunted
houses and things that turn you upside down,
and ate a slice of doughy pizza near a slide.
We saw dangerous riding exercises,
competitions penning cattle (all the men
succeeded, all the women failed) and awards
for polished tack. So much mastery over beasts,
so much of being human; nature very near
and very far. By dusk I had it sorted out

as boring, almost painful; we'd had enough,
though as we reached the car again
four terribly handicapped children
were just arriving to be part of this,
wheeled in carts, eyes fixed on the darkening
sky or the pillow, the lights or nothing.
And so, we met another vision
of the body's possibilities and of our luck,
our precious luck, and of this community,
this celebration of winnings, strengths and
transformations we had wished not even
to imagine. And perhaps it's real,
the lot; perhaps these carers really know.

In the City of Niagara, for Example

For Brian and Katrina Shaver (and Gretchen)

So I don't work here but I can see
it's the real stuff. It's got to have heat –
so clusters of steel chimneys and flared off
gasses and orange light as though in a
permanent, gathering thunder storm.
It works behind the scenes of the pretty worlds,
the honeymoon attractions. I'd like to speed
through it, though the Boulevard is in a 35 zone
(between the Factory Outlet Mall and the Falls)
in this wonderful, heavy, air-conditioned car.
The air seems better down residential Walnut
and over Nineteenth, Seventeenth, Fifth, First;
quickly back to the water, parks and farms.
I open the car door. A dog barks again and again.
The sound is clear and uncomfortable. It sticks
hard in the air. Or I'd like it to. Precisely,
there between the trees. But it is without such
compromise and it vanishes. The ironies come clean,
facile and unloveable. The dog barks
again and again for all she's worth.

Sunset on the Lake

The sun and the horizon slowly close
and squeeze the great circles of gold to meet
the mist on the lake's lifted, softening edge.
Half-purple cat's eye narrowing for its
catch: night-light, the barred, scabby waves under
the dulling sun-track. Relentlessly, the
flies fountain above the water, touch and
release; a million little triggers, for
the blessing of an animal's quick death.
So the lake eases into its unseen
power, the flaking, gold path drenches away
into flat, black oils. The flies' gush dissolves
towards the shore and nothing takes its place.
The dark body cools; a soundless clearing.

Chrysalis

For us to watch
with our passions,
our love
of transformations
and time for
the coming day.
Drab, outlined
wings; red
bloated club
of a body;
flightless tiny
sphinx; the head
sculpted with
blank eyes;
mask true
to its outgrowing.
When the heat comes
it lives
for itself,
squirming, splitting;
cast off,
like an old question,
the case now
is almost clear,
essentially broken.
The new thing grows
past the dew,
leaves, dark
tree skin. In
the light,
good and quick
as a storm cloud.
Without us.
Thunder.
And such lightning
is there
unannounced.

Glass

What the creek had been like in winter was hard
to tell. In midsummer it started as a band of trees
curving through the rectangular fields. Piped
under roads it spilled again as a rift of wild creep-
ers, strong, gray grasses and crowns of nettles.
In late August there lasted out in the ancient
forest a few puddles sinking in after yesterday's
thunder-storm; some used up by the algae and
gels, some still clear.

Water-insects handle
the surface tension
with curious skill

as though moulding warm
blown glass; a pliable
world that does what

it's told for now and
for these soft creatures
left alone in the setting

earth. The sun works on
towards mid-day, jealous
of the last wet places:

its success taunted by
gourd-skins and small, blue
butterflies dancing

and resting for the sake
of their sweet knowledge:
flowers and air, transient,

fluid territories kissed
in flurries of perfection.
Under this evaporating prize

the turtles believe their
depth and clam up the worst
heart-beats. It's nearly over;

condensed illumination steadies
down. Two red-tailed hawks
silence it all, try elsewhere.

Things Change Colour

Fir trees' young branches, for example,
a perfect blue, like deep ice,
and they persist as winter's proudest
possessions, burgeoning needles of frost,
in the late Spring. And they settle
for the green of last year and the year
before, dull backdrop to the hot, clear
songs of new birds; to a goldfinch,
to a lost tropical storm. Each over-
worked season's dye washed out to deceive
and cleanse a landscape.
                          Pictures defy it
all, summary provenance of helpless vision,
hearts moving to a stop. We won't have it,
we won't even remember. Clear sunflowers.

And so the Blue Sky Again

Oh, these fields and the dense forests; so much
of civilization and its pastoral contents.

And writing thus, things harden their demands even
in lovely summer sunshine: describe it all for love,

for mankind, for the last perfection, for the untended
left-over worlds that might shrivel before night;

describe it so it makes sense, even as it opens
and opens like a gigantic window whose frame fades

way out of sight, but yet it opens so wide the jealous,
haphazard pictures pale and stretch to nothingness.

Sweet failures. Arcadia here for the price of a word
or silence or anything worth doing.

And so the blue sky again.

Angry Birdsong

Have you heard such pain?
More public than the crass
jealousies that mark us
(glances, boredom) and threading
between territories with
scentless razor-wires of sound.
Any transgression invokes
these infinitely beautiful
arts of self-preservation.
Nothing like our museums or
meanings (stony dungeons,
glass cases for bandaged,
anointed mummies of our
ancestors). To achieve all
that, the empty spaces audibly
betokened, (fly, fly), and
dividing or attracting
with vibrant, sleek exchange
of blood (or for blood):
unanswerable, quick languages
forever in the present tense.

Pookie

For Nancy Shaver

Pookie went out in the fields and then she had a tick. It
was evening and the nearest vet was seventeen miles.
Diseases of the brain we thought, and fits. A firm grip
under the skin. And you mustn't break off or it's gone in
and finally. So we asked Ken and he said to heat a match
red hot quickly before it was too deep. So that.

And the tick flaring its blood
along the hot match. Its hooked
encounters with the other lives
now relax. It grows, outgrows.
Hot scab; a painful communion
fails and heals after waiting
so long in the grass like
knowledge, like what happens

and under, beneath layer
upon layer of ancient surgeons'
knives and probes, arrowheads
from deeper strata, archeology
upturns all the other body-
invaders that shaped our past:
curved, blunt blades to scrape
the cleansing olive oil,
the pin for a weeping ear.

Such crafty instruments of
pleasure and catastrophe;
the metallic, disruptive shapes
of what our clumsy flesh
seemed to want; a brief, flaming
theatre of incision for you alone.

Windows

A wasp hesitates
an unprepared tunnel
light to an inner world
but closed and still

the wasp dances
to the centre and back
the centre and up
and there dust
and webs

     gone
to more fluid entries
to the strong perfumes
to the centre and trees

drops of clear resin
the pines' swelling
soft windows
light unlocked

I am sitting at a table in the garden. From the kitchen door, behind me, two women come, dressed in blue, one to the left, one to the right, for flowers perhaps, or to the garbage. They buffet the set colours aside into wild planes of light, vanish behind the shed, (the white paint is peeling, clearly), and the grass awakens into translucency, each step bereft, but dancing, as though behind green glass.

And the Sky

And the sky clearing after rain,
three white butterflies whirl
past the edge of the trees
to the blue-flowered field,

and all the sounds change.
Like a door opening,
the rooms widen, and,
if there are crickets

they are singing together
as if there were no traps
and no end to the heat
and the air that feeds them.

And so, new shadows; the prized
darks where the grass tries some more.

Looking for the Salt Spring Again

The forest floor was clear and undisturbed
apart from fallen nuts and scattered four-
leafed seedlings. Grey, thin-stemmed trees grew high to
canopies of leaves, sunlit, pale and sharp.

A track wove in and out of the forest
edge from field to wood and field again where
vines and grasses joined. And then the creekside
clearing, walled by flowers and bright, cascading

weeds. I crossed the dry creek bed and trod
on mint and carefully passed the feathery
nettles' seven foot bouquets. Behind these
energetic falls, fountains and flakes of

radiant thistledown the well was partly
hidden, the ancient clearing almost full
with luxuries beyond all human gifts.
The upturned log was greyer, streaked and frail,

colours faded, and grass had reached its rim.
Two frogs rested, waiting, on a stick that
cut the high clouds' clear, reflected surface,
and flicked at flies that drifted down to meet

the distant salty water through the sky.
That final, deep, mysterious lens was
far below the level of the ground as
though, like an extended telescope, its

images adjusting to clarity,
focussed but retreating to a smaller
world, it needed no more light. The Indians'
well-preserved fish and meat may vanish from

the forest's tangible world, reduced to
tiny crystals by the creek, their wooden
walls invisible, but simply there for
the mind, bending the light just how you need

to the line of sight of the older ones,
intelligence drawn after it. You're gone.

Late Evening 11th August

Colours left,
the Earth breathed out.
Trees, in the closing
blackness, were points
of insect sound
and nothing more.

A wider space above
and measured out
in dots and floods
of certain light,
quite silent, rich
and unpossessed.

Why watch, why ask?
And meteors, their
scored and spreading
light, so quick and sure,
etched near an angle
unexpected, lost.

Such final partings,
burned up, faceless atoms;
to be sure they do not scream
and have no music:
if this is trust
or love or anything

we draw in our pictures,
our daylight?
Our happy predictions?
The system spinning?
And science, our annual
flowers, our beauty?

Moving On

The wind was cool
although it was from the South.
It came as a noise of breathing,
of long hair being combed,
of the sea digging.

And the smell of the forest
waved and sighed
from one tree to the next
and stopped as the air
touched my ears, my neck

like a delicate, cold
invisible hat
that settled itself, closely,
for a second and then
blew away. I heard

only what was moving on,
the unrehearsed mime
in your head, the relief,
the silent ways of saying
goodbye in a thunder-storm.

Summer Fog

A line of trees dripping in summer fog;
so curious the surfaces, like a kiss,
like a hug after a year apart, like
people, and all they've got, meeting again

for what seems the last time. Tears work between;
boundaries smudge with noises that seem to have
inhabited their own world but now slip
and pivot on the glistening leaves

on a journey from clearing to clearing,
looping and dipping like a purple finch,
free. Heart beats. The dew and mist unfurl
like a giant grey flower that drops to the ground

at the end of its season, and the air
is clear again, draws back from its crying;
it has become self-sufficient. But, still
pleading for some infinite love, the colours

glow and sharpen. At least to be remembered:
so divided, so callous, so casual.

Here Is Rain

Here is rain. Since seven this morning
the house roof and the leaves and flowers
have been speaking, catching breath,
the air's heavy water transported

in green channels and white sprays
to my ears: words. Easy, easy.
Rose heads, spent and washed of beauty;
the scent falls out in the dripping light

and birdsong weighs it and lifts it –
so many gifts spun out generously
into the grass. Listen. Across the road,
on the other side of the field, are two horses.

They flick their tails. There's a low, light-
green bush near tall trees and the grey dome
of a corn silo. There is no final way to see it,
though it seems good enough like this, to be

moist and unhurried; an image working steadily
throughout the sparkling gels of an enormous,
charmed eye where there's space for everything.
Birds' wings whir nearby, through and beyond the words.

Or all speaking, spoken for? Shy or crafty?
It is beyond trying.

The Illuminated Forest

It was soon after sunrise,
and the light met the forest edge
horizontally so illuminating

those tunnels the birds take,
the insects' lofts and decks.
There was surprising light

on the underside of leaves,
and pine-needles counted out
the night's rain in sprays of silver.

The new season's cones dried
with springy blobs of resin,
a bejewelled dress unstitched

unworn, unwarmed. As the sun rose
higher the whole thing darkened
and closed as though it had been

inside out and now the proper view
of it was re-established, concealed,
dull and precious, a body re-dressed.

Flies danced and buzzed around my neck
and arms and ankles to seal it off,
to say what they wanted from me

to be sure of their possessions,
crying, crying, wanting the words
to fail. Or, as you might say,
now, the bereaved were speechless.

Lichen

One piece of lichen obsessed me.
There was a low branch
that curved out into the sunlight

its dark and silver-green needles
alive to the torrent of flies
and dripping gum. On its bark

the lichen was rough, like a tiny
sea, with waves and points
and curled edges, or paint

on a canvas just millimetres thick
but light went on through it,
reflecting back from every ring

of the tree's growth, through years,
through every tide, seasons' ends,
blanks. I looked at it. One morning

I counted seven sorts of flies
visiting the tree, the usual
wasps and bees and one brilliant

odd insect with a long, white tail.
I was far from here. I was drawn
as if by capillary attraction

through these stems and tunnels
and branches. I was near the mist
in the flies' wings,

the blue-grey lichen dust,
near the insects' tongues
touching something in order to live.

Gourd Vine

Tiresome, tireless, it's gotten all over the compost heap.
Its long-throated, yellow flowers trick themselves out
beneath great, bland ragged leaves; and the new gourds
awaiting their identity in curls and blotches of green
and brown. It's so sure of its random paths, of its
sources of warm food. It's so much like the love we have
for the earth: fragrant, shady and kind. Or might have had.
Just think of the power station down the road,
of our cost-effective Industrial Heritage Parks, of the
Museums of Labour History.
                              Last month we paid to see
pale effigies of workers with TB lying five to a bed
in a North Country re-constructed mine. These sports
of our tolerant imagination riot over the real spoil heaps,
and make their mark, oh, so gently
                                    like the filtered shade
of the licensed smoke-stack waste, the falling pine needles,
the things we make heroic and necessary (the suffering
in former centuries) and gardens that we strive to cultivate
into patterns of colour and produce, the forms and flowers
we seem to need beyond, beside, our deaths.
                              Oh love, this and this alone.

The Milkweed Field

The milkweed field – and
other flowers too, so many crazy
hats at different angles (no-one could
possibly be talking to each other

or listening). Grand, sunlit, private
languages hovering four feet above
the ground – yellow, white and blue
words to be sucked into brief

coherence by clouds of butterflies,
by storms, by the dashing rains;
what homes, what grammar, what
cutlery, body lotions and typefaces.

Cloud

The high storm cloud passed eastwards on the lake
and missed us. Angular and bright edged it held
a moment's power, great currents of water
and electric shifts, hidden flues and cables.

It was something to watch as its side carved
the sun from our half of the sky and it
towered on like the wall of an Atlantic
liner, black and stable. It's strange

such threats, demanding our attention and
gratitude, still live on in Latin names
and metaphor – 'cumulo-nimbus' and
'anvil-shaped' – no simple word for that quite

dangerous, unmeasurable mountain
of water drops and air. A brilliant sunset.
Now the road is dry, words close up again
into a tasteful interior décor.

Calligraphy

Knowing what has happened: a tree, a mill-race,
a nest. The crucial desires and bribes. Bitter
professional re-writing of great wars.

Love the neat craft of ideas, payment by results,
meanings teased to a stop: such flourishing
visions graft to the senseless particles,

their genius matched up to hot paradise
or dreams of harrowing, rare earths. And learned:
the parts of the flower, textual names, half-lives.

Learned: the sub-atomic dusts in the dark.
Thus. Documentary: for death – make it
as good as you can; for bending light – gnaw

at it; for absolute zero – cross it
through; for love – the lucid background – paper,
papyrus, draw it to you like water.

Before Babel

Swallowing their live water.
Jeffrey Wainwright

A friend sent us a post card from the *Musée
Historique des Tissus* in Lyon: a tapestry
of the Third or Second Century from
Coptic Egypt; in fragments – but with precise,
almost photographic detail – there were fish,
muscled and golden, spaced evenly in
the fabric as though, so appropriate,
already on exhibition (or for sale),
the cloth thicker where the fish were woven
into the background (back-cloth) and so
preserved, whilst much of the surrounding weave
(sandy, earth-coloured) had perished; lithe, fluent,
inhuman and free, like birds of some Paradise
uncontained by language, by ideas, by gunnery.

To sink through this,
forever swimming
into light; to feel
the needle and thread
(as it were) cutting
the waves, repeating
scales and fins and spines
(justice: a cool,
fine pressure
on my finger); to be, thus,
mindless and unearthed,
just as water might flood
the blood-packed gills:
oxygen firing and fired on
from cell to cell,
all drawing the words (rather
'works') for battle
into suspension and
delight as though still, and
without tears, before Babel.

Fire Place

Old wells, old mines, old chimneys;
transports, stills of desire,
dug for water, for the brittle,
tardy minerals, for the air,
for this humane consumption.

Leaf-veins split in the hearth,
the trees' black minds sizzle
and scatter ancient heats – for us,
for our brief, inviting pressures,
billowing to the decorated pot

near Orion. Mill wheels. Mill wheels.
Families stretch their toes towards
the hearth, the chimney's fragrant dust,
lank clinker of commemoration.
The children grow.

The Vase

I dropped the vase and just had time to kick it sideways
before it reached the floor: a gesture to savour, or save,
for its hopeless, human co-ordination. It rolled away, the
rim sprang apart, its bold curves upending their values,
geometries and colours. And, for this occasion, its own
perfect sounds skip and dizzy over the tiles. Forever
untuning, the shivers rock still and that harmony out-
pours in clicks, in spaces, in a threadless release. Craft
and sadness spread thinly into silence; the lush ceramics
and warm glaze too good to hold.

On the grass, the last
of the morning's dew;
a lens unskilled
in brief surface tension,

the hypnotic meniscus
of gravity's playful
vision to see through.
A wasp tugs the grassblade,

dabbing and tonguing
the liquids as they distil
along the wings' buzzing,
the sting, the juice,

into the myriad, flawless
eyes. Flowers suck and
display in the deep un-
coagulated, mid-day light.

Locks

Locking the door – once, twice –
to guard the money and passports
cheques and plastic. To command
these complex, oiled barrels

a unique, ground edge, nicely
turned. Thus, the brass is primed
and falls into its dedicated
socket; a slow, reversible

bullet-journey immobilizing doors,
territories, artworks, trash.
All this safe? And to hold
with an irreplaceable, coded key –

like light?
              Sun, shade – colours
cover and search each tree
and grassblade, loving, like
a tangible amnion, tracing

the darkest pits of foliage
and beneath the undercells
of mushrooms, quick-witted
night-time growths. Leaves free

their paler surfaces to the wind
and waves of heat hasten
each insect's voyage through
the bright houses of birdsong,

perfume and uncut timber.
Even the night rests open, and,
however far from us, the stars,
uncluttered and unspaced
allow for light.

Pet Shop

For Rhiannon

For the mind's fortune, the young,
inept and dangerous creatures
of comfort reveal what we can approach
to love. Day-old blind mice and an angry
cockatoo to be touched if you dare,
if you want it enough. Cages of insects
and electric-blue fish,
the illumination of our rough, unkempt
fears, a peep-show so complete
and undiseased that we needn't attend
the deaths backstage in this deep,
fluorescent, urban mall.
Fifty cent crickets sing in
perpetual daylight, safe for now amongst
the exposed bright vermin of the sea.

Archeology

Pretty things as I've wanted them.
Old bones, shells, fragments of cloth
so replete with knowledge. Thus. Any.
Make it the stuff of culture,
fine patterns, lost colours, the hours of work,
the dedication, (fear, perhaps),
mazes of metal and ink, pigments roughly
fired, the flickers and shards of war
(wars?). The past spills out its goods,
accounts to carry forward, superfluous
digits, the numbers believed in
for their own sake, too, to witness
what might (still) be perfection.

And above my head, fighter planes
on training exercises fly all morning
north-eastwards, accelerate with a scream
of engines, turn 180° and return to base,
all invisible in the low cloud. I know
they're there and, I suppose, what they're doing,
(safe?) for a version of the past,
some future, too, for awful revelation.

Dishes

Putting away the dishes,
they are clean, (they wake us,
they are bright); to their places,
places. This crowded, stacked

order you dance to, stabbing
into drawers and cupboards,
it is there for now, the way
of things. Through the wall,

beyond these wooden frames
and the blue and white, kiln-fired
patterns of nature
is something else that needs feeding,
day and night, without regrets.

Old Clothes

That decision to throw it away – crap;
the worn out. Too small, too grey, too
much cloth in the wrong place. It's
intolerable, it takes up too much room,
it's in the corner of my eye
and it needs to go;

like a vision that once suited everything,
like sitting at the kitchen window, quite
alone with a coffee, the mosquito repellant
(that won't come out, and I'm not going outside
until) and the humming-bird
at the feeder outside, sipping,

twenty three sips I counted and each time
it looked up and around and the sun caught its
red throat like flashing marble from a distant
hillside, or gunfire – so shocking and quick –
yet, there it was, for an instant quite still;
attention-seeking, a balance
always needing to be redressed.

Chest of Drawers

I ask you – what use this painted, over-
painted, scratched hulk? Bubbled and chipped
grey over red over white over wood. Perhaps
simply that: priceless, cast off
shell of someone's possessions (so ours) –
like the worn clothes themselves; a show,
a surface, a framework as rough
and unpredictable as shadow; acknowledged
hiding place, our camouflaged, bland, neutral
territory. In there, the identities
that fall like grass. In smooth running
drawers and loose hinges the repeated
daily actions of all emptying bodies
sorted out. Our lost souls' instructions
and shapes; unusable. A collector's item; so.

Scars

This is the tissue
that we grow into.
Faceless keloid,
stiff, sweatless putty;
it blots over
the deeper wounds,
unjoinable pipes
and endings.
Weeping poison-ivy skin
dries printlessly
into it; the cuts
of glass, of surgery;
pock marks. Our
second flesh
that holds us

when all else fails;
like sounds
from the perfect world:
all the distant birdsong
and the deep forest
animals' ferocious
gnawing. Rejoicing,
the nameless elements
get louder
offering these scars
for us to love now.

Bite

And the mosquitoes aren't so bad this morning.
The grass is dry in spite of yesterday's rain.
And no dew, either. It's clear and the wind's
from the North though that doesn't matter

when you're moving. The light's good and old
and knowledgeable; it's almost too tight
and sharp to walk through. It seems to tug
like a hairbrush. It's along my fingers, cutting

like a kite-string, drawing fiercely towards
the sun. Reds and greens are close to hand, jagged
and unmixed, still self-possessed as a fresh bite –
risks, riches, calculations – under my skin.

Devil's Hole

The sound of a saw
on the wind.
Mile upon mile.
Creatures fall
in our path.

Trees, the years'
survivors, bend
their obedience.
Mosquitoes, hummingbirds.
The whir of memories.

Retreat. Pardons,
seals, torn contracts.
Insect bites adrift
in their universe.
Spinning for a million

years round their loved
probe. A chance intersection
of shadows; total eclipse.
Itch. Itch.
From the window

the garden expands;
rank on rank of colours
rushing to the sun.
Pitiless exchange.
The gorge pleads

as the English troops
crumble in,
horses still switching
at flies; hell bent
on justice; silence
bartered and dissolved
away like red salt.

Fort George, Fort Niagara, Fort Mississauga

Not a word out of place.
Nor grass, nor varnished cannon.
Palisades, embankments
and viewing platforms

(see Vauban in North America)
skim the wars we might care
to forget in battle order
adjusted to our time

so merry and quaint
to be rewarded and re-told;
the muskets on the hour
fired, lead shot melted

and recast, uniforms beloved
and stitched in time for us
the untouchable visitors
who will make of it what we want

and what we need and so retreat
into the outside undefended,
natural wordless place.
Past the walls, past tears.

Orders to the Niagara Frontier

Whichever George or Louis paid for these forts
strung through new worlds of disputed waste, trees,
rivers and coastline? Seems beside the point;
they must have been cracked. Three hundred miles
of forest and then a tiny clearing, palisade,
guardroom and armoury to be defended, or not,
depending on the weather, supplies and disease.

And 'orders' (sealed papers, bound language,
like poems with the closure of death or freedom
or neglect or irrelevance); the words that won't
translate, the metaphors split like some crumbling,
outworn, impressed wax – so the kings are dead
and the frontiers moved ('Defend it at all
costs for the greater glory of your . . .'). So what.

Imagine opening the letters long after they were
signed, perhaps six months after, after the snow
had settled, after you had learned they had their god,
too, after their language seemed to work and
you were glad to hear their children shouting
from across the field. Your skin had done itching
and your clothes were black and greased like leather.

Imagine the new orders, being written now, for you
to get in six more months if you hadn't died or run
or changed your name or your country. Well, they were
the stuff of literature for Fenimore Cooper
already as they dropped into disuse. Images
that became too real, that needed cultivation
and preservation, again, at all costs. And the wars

of Europe slither on, dividing, unkillable, round
valleys and forests and defensible hills, round
a strategic town. The orders keep coming to light
even after so long, this long, when those garrisons
and camps and histories seemed all lost, unpronounceable
names in the comforting, deathless past. Dead metaphors,
and without compassion? I fear. I fear the frozen,
travelling words. And I never knew such distances.

An Art of War

For Jon Silkin

A door closes; and, yes, I can hear the
chisel on marble (like footsteps, like sighs)
retribution clicking against the stone.
Urban gatherings, mineral conquests,

a living town aroused into praise and
decoration, in that nagging language
which, they say, writes us. The British Museum
holds so many wars transfixed (and hunts, races)

in stone, Greek chariots crashing into
the unnerved people, and their arms entangled
for the sake of someone's composition
with horses' legs and leather strapping,

the forged, muscular coats of uniformed
imprisonment. And Assyrian lions
harassed into the closed rooms of our own
disgusting glory; imperial rooms

spat out, the dizzying outcasts and rough
asides of words, grammar and gifts of the
rich ones to our culture. So, what will we
choose to place inside such rooms amongst the

glass and electronics, the virtual
realities we might endow to the
heritage? To leave in controled heat and
artificial light, named and patronised?

From Vietnam, the Falklands, the Gulf and
Bosnia (coming home, it seems) we will
learn to love, what, their transience? Perhaps
their awful sophistication, the powered,

binary, language that organises
surgical strikes and clears each hospital
of drugs and water and anaesthetics.
This instant, microchip mail renders up

the art of war (armour) we have worked on
so long. A programmed, pin-point war poetry
seeded in computer games, diversions
in which just anything is possible

to pass the time. And pain might be subsumed
in clever art; the language, set free, will
surely allow for that easy way out,
for speech without regret yet in control,

and sight, without compassion, whatever
your finger tips might trace along the jaws
and open wounds, the shattering filigree
of veins and bones, alone, beside themselves.

Jelly Fish

They pulse without rhythm or surprise
like anatomical sections in formalyn
coming to their own awful life,
sloughed from some ancient, discarded,
transparent body. Their world hangs
through rocks, earth and sand; they ride
the currents through time, through ages
of heat and cold, beyond the continents'
built-up edges. Their own boundaries seem
internalised: curled, blue quarters,
like the fringes of iris petals,
mark the skinless flesh.
For water, to water; an unbleeding
gel in the sea's own deathless,
multiple eyes, spawning without
vanity in the sea's full view.
Satisfied with survival, their salty
but tearless sockets drift apart
and they settle for any depth
of the cloudless Atlantic's swell;
their plastic, unmuscled futures
tumble into unimagined clarity.

Words

I was trying to stretch my legs, shuffling
towards the back of the TriStar, somewhere
in mid-Atlantic. I had a middle seat,
so no views from there – just the wings and flaps
and the whole thing flexing during turbulence.
'If you want a good look, try the little window
in the door at the rear.' I thanked the attendant,
who was smoking avidly between the lunch
and the duty-frees, moved to the emergency door,
(that flimsy, plastic-covered lever, oxygen,
loud-hailer), and peered through the tiny, thick pane.
Those queueing for the toilets looked the other way.
The sea, from six miles up, still seemed rippled
and wavey – to appear like that from up here
I must have been seeing the great shapes
of ocean swell, patterns within patterns, miles across.
The glass made rainbows and distortions.

Next time
we were over Ontario – lakes, rivers, forests;
some sort of creation there for the asking. Perhaps
still un-mapped, I hoped, and feared. I returned
to my seat and buckled in for the final descent,
and chewed hard to release the pressure in my ears.
Wordless, unimagined places seemed stuck there
between my jawbones and eardrums (all those gluey
ducts, hammer, anvil, stirrup, the fluids and canals
of meaning). I imagined a surgeon carefully uncovering
those tiny structures to allow our well-known sounds
to enter a silent inner world, and, for a moment,
I was in a place without sense, containing the rush of air,
simply, waiting for names and an awakening.

Taxi

11.00 pm in a taxi heading for the lake
and downtown Toronto from the airport.
To the left, the high-lit towers and all around
the points and chains of light that mark
more roads. It had all been below us minutes before
coming down through the clouds; so much concrete
and electricity to clear the way for touchdown
after the icebergs way out in the ocean,
the frost and endless forests. Our eyes are drawn
to the tallest structure made by man (at least
till now), a modern staging post. The taxi
seems silent after eight hours in a Tristar.
We are tired and the driver only speaks Spanish.
The road is wide and clear and he's speeding.
The air-conditioning hums and apart from headlights
and taillights and windows there are no signs
of people (as though we are still flying
privately, lazily above the world).
But, just before we turn hard left to the
C N Tower the smell of skunk squeezes
and cools into the car's red velvet interior;
the real, indefatigable smell of welcome
to North America (that must be all around,
drifting through the safe, residential
city certainties). Maybe it had just been
killed by a car or was fighting off a suburban
pet to protect its young. Whatever, we're
happy to have arrived. Our hotel
is air-conditioned and we fall asleep,
our free shampoos and bath gels quite untouched,
the complimentary perfumes of the new
world good enough to combat jet-lag and the
Atlantic's restless spaces with something
animal, warm and comforting.

The Roman Aqueduct is Still in Use

Above the unfit earth, memorialised
as a worthwhile result (solution),
like a thought, like mathematics,

these stones arch over the tortured
and their rough, expendable thirst.
The idea of water here comes home

in solid style where uplifted carving
civilises enforced pain, democratic cries,
flesh serving flesh for its calculated

weight. A sort of destiny bestowed
to be forgotten enlarges on the slaves
who built it so that a trickle

of water might still accustom itself
to the high channel, invisible currents
answer the sunlight in thrilling

imagination like the waters in Hell,
or the cliff-face of sea at the old
world's edge. Only the grief leaks

from these tons of rock ordered once
to end thirst and to start it.

Landscape of Pleasure

This flat land is learned with humanity,
its lights and silts panned out as though by a
first, victorious gravity, its dams,
polders and windmills become a proper
world of wounds and adaptations. The sea
pumped down, earth glassed over to cultivate
tomatoes' marketable quality. Acres
of artificial reflection, the sun's
cull, materialised. Delft's blue and white
unnatural clarity, a basic
rock rendered and dished as something to eat
off, as something to consume, smoothing the
flooded pits of war, North Sea's and armies'
fatal accommodation. Sciences
settle the end of Europe's estuary.

But higher: the Rhine's distant origins,
slipping snow and rock-falls, brilliant meadows
and quick shadows. A landscape of trial and
error unwanted for art or battle,
nudging away such confiding realisms
without contentment or artful vision,
growing like a rattler out of its skin.

Cave

The air was soft at first and then edgy and cool. I found myself breathing deeply and listening, as though it might soon be lost, compacted to rock-born bubbles or re-absorbed into the porous, dribbling walls. A vacuum might seem more natural to contain this effortless stroll through the ground, on paths of spent rivers and cracked strata of ice-age weight. I should be forbidden. My steps don't echo; the air gives back nothing that doesn't belong.

> The rock's shining, temperate fluid
> outloves us. Through the millenia
> a hall of mirrors bends its slow
> shapes to perfection. Slippery
> creams of stone fill out the air,
> fill out the light, setting in
> silence the murderous growths
> of our beginnings. A harbour
> in gravity's swing, its mouth
> bedecked with flowers and distant
> lichens of perpetual half-dark.
> The earth's secret, constant art;
> our scents and hopes excluded,
> bring it your bones, your tender eyes,
> your moisture – whatever.

Timing

I stayed in a village where the one church clock struck out each hour twice over, just before and just after (I imagined) the agreed divisions of sixty minutes. The trim echoes (but which was of which?) were both comic and insistent: a reminder that time was clearly passing or an attempt to slow it down. Between each chime a sort of No Man's Time when anything might, or might not, happen. Was it an accident of manufacture, a theological conflict or did some inventive clock-maker patent this mechanism, dreaming and considering his powers?

A tractor path edges the field
through hard sloughs of mud
and golden plants waiting to give up
their season's work to watchful

human keepers. Well-trodden ways
divide the hedgerows, forests,
untreated soil and lucky, if
haphazard, weeds. Here, justly

grounded, the craft of predicting
brightest autumn sugars,
dark vines and the first deep
roots close to the winter rain.

Love, frost: to know the Earth's
turning, such awful wants.

Moving

The picture is of dust
finally in love.
Archeologists dig
and brush for a lifetime
to reach this intimate
but dry kiss
on the neck.
Radius and ulna
weigh almost nothing
over her hip:
all those lasting
differences of
his texture and
feeling: so deathly
light and matter
of fact. Composed:
two skeletons
show up to the light
as though painted
with yellow strokes
on one level surface,
nudge the chances
of our modern pleasure;
they move into the sand,
into each other,
as deftly as sea-
creatures burying
themselves just
for the time being.

The Goldshops of Hydra

Miniature, splendid security:
O metal, metal! Ringed and beaten
to match an absent love; these
silent joints and pictures, clever

chains splayed on the model plush
and velvet. All history of vacant
flesh rolls out of the workshop
crucible on to these sunlit counters,

becoming the franchised wealth
of beauty; the markers of our nerves
and disparate surfaces, the promises
of pleasure inverted into free

minerals and the earth's rare
atoms polished for all they're
worth. A cold décor for now;
a precious solid clasped.

Glass Goblet

From another age – I don't remember –
say, Roman or Renaissance. To drink
the transparent water from such stony
hollows: such quiet, unbounded thirst

to be filled, to be seen and be seen through,
a love uncharted and yet cradled in
two hands, there, a composite lens unfocussed
but offering the glass-blower's gift of

spring flowers to your lips, painted and streaked
with decorative impurities like
his blood, and ancient, bubbled parasites,
the ingested dull venom of his words for

beauty, and ours, so deeply bitten in
colours of his proud attempts at faithful
reproduction of nature. To hold our
drink, poor, stately flowers, in clearing veins

of blue and white and green (petals grown from
drifts of moist snowdrop bulbs shining somewhere
distant, like soft and sea-washed bottle shards
ground between black pebbles) drawn and cut from

the white-hot chemicals, cooled and pressed into
service. So, giving up cloudy leaves and
stalks that cry out for words, liquid tongues, a
condensing and hurrying flood where the

light seems not to stop. One flick of a finger
nail and it hums quietly and waves of sunshine
break over it and through it but, no, daring
guile beyond pleasure, it simply won't speak.

Leaves

There is one tree near the end of the garden
whose leaves are large with a pale underside.
So that when the wind blows the whole thing
becomes lighter and it shimmers like dull,
green gold. And then they clap and rattle

with the sounds of the sea sucking through shingle
or slow, fragile horses drawing the wind.

On the very first French farm where we camped
(the family in 1952)
was a row of such trees beside my tent.
There, in the leaves, the Channel waves all night
and the cliff-side of the ferry to stare down,

the sun and the wake turning in patterns
of green and blue, strong foam prickling under

the dark hull and sighing to the same gulls
all the way to Dunkirk. The waves journeyed
from side to side of the tent, flapping the
canvas wall and rushing on to the next field.
I was left, not sleeping, I was sure, in

a pool of silence until the next approach
of watery leaves, the exotic world,

taste of boiled milk ('pas de café pour les
enfants, monsieur') and the unthinkable
stretch of time without Baked Beans. The farmer
offered us brandy next morning, still glad
to see the British, and a tour of the farm.

I remember a main road which cut through
the farm-yard (slurry on the car wheels that night),

a dog leashed under a cart to pull it,
panting, scrawny and working, and a man
kicking a horse ('don't look'), and here, small, foul,
milky-smelling sheds of tiny calves, white.
As we were bundled out and back to the

kitchen, a still empty glass curled up in
my hand, I asked, 'Veal?' with all the guilt and

excitement that attends something sensed to
be cruel. We drove on through grey villages,
their walls flaking and pock-marked ('by the War'),
to another farm and boiled milk and
more tough bread. It was, I suppose, like all

holidays, a priceless voyage into
freedom and knowledge – places in which

we may foresee what might become habits
of a lifetime, the gifts that still scare
and outlive the eyes and ears as they
dull and sicken. Until they're all that's left
to be handed on, though they're neither mute nor

indifferent: pain to be consumed, or
outstared, beneath all the warning voices.

Bringing up the Past

Our holiday brochure said there were the ruins of a Mycenaen city at one end of the beach as well as the night life and good food. We picked it. And, indeed, the ruins were there, singularly ignored: a rocky hill dropping straight into the sea. A few hundred yards from the apartments, past two bars and the pedaloes, a track led through the lemon trees to the beginnings of a wall. The hill's smoother contours had been sharpened and built up for defence several times since 1000 BC and as we climbed above the increasingly symmetrical stones Rhiannon nearly slipped through the top of what must have been a beehive tomb excavated 100 years before by the Germans and left to heather and thyme and the odd beer can glowing in a shaft of sunlight. Perhaps bring a torch tomorrow? No guides, no signs, no guidebooks. Really best left. Though, indeed the best sort of ruin. Abby climbed to the top in slippery sandals and shivered. Elaine had packed the rucksack with an English picnic which she spread out at 1.00 p.m. We joked about Homer and the fleet setting off past here for Troy. Rhiannon produced a book from her pocket (*The Passion*, I think), and read with her back to the tombs and wouldn't move further. It was the one cloudy day and we glanced furtively at the half-deserted beach below. We did what we wanted; we were, for a time somewhere else. Though next day, sunny again, I swam round to it with a snorkel and mask.

For the eyes' sake,
a tempered glass frame
to my purchased, seaside
underworld. The smeary,
blinkered beach-chairs
and bathers, already
overcrowded, became
smaller, disappeared,
left living on the
surface, and, with this mask
I sank just inches down
to another roofless, half-
inhabited world of fish
and sand and coral and slowly

moved to the deeper water.
The rippling weed
and pebbles soon shelved
down beyond my depth
and then a clear-cut edge
of rock ran out and there
showed no solid surface,
just the blue, soft light,
and there, below
and between my fingers
the silent, motionless fish
hanging by the line of a cliff
in some sightless, incalculable,
precious order, like the leaves
on a row of trees glittering
as far as the eye could see.

I looked out of the water
once towards the distant,
stony city and swam on,
along the fishes' track
across the bay. Until,
out of the bottomless haze,
another line of rocks appeared;
the tumbled, rough-hewn harbour's
edge emerged through sand
and shingle and sparkled
in the sun. Just above me,
the higher cliff and lichen
and herbs where we had all
walked; below and all around,
the clear red blobs of sea
anemones and cast off urchin shells
(like skulls beneath the walls?)
and fish, the loveliest,
safest, living occupants.

So long as the mask held true
beneath the sea the ancient city
breathed a sort of after-life
with quiet Hades' creatures
near and real and undeserved.

But the salt was near my eyes.
I sniffed and spat and dived
for an urchin shell before
returning: a skein of minerals
washed and rubbed from the hand-
carved rocks – to hold its patterns
and fragile joints, to hold
like a dull, hollow jewel offered
from an unrobbed tomb.
I dived, spashing and unskilled,
again and again until I caught
a shell without crushing it,
and I turned, spluttering and cold
to swim, one-handed, through the bay.

I reached the beach, heavy
and short-sighted. The urchin shell
dried in a moment, leaving dusty
soil to blow away, to kiss.
The colours faded, drama and battle
disarmed, and, reluctantly,
I settled for the shades the sun
goes on with. Though I wanted it
to speak, simply and just to me,
like a message in a bottle
from someone unlocateable
or long since dead,
but coming again to life.
I imagined the words awakening
behind a mask – quick and expressive
and true, but still enough to touch.

Domestic History

For Robin and Linda Glover

A house of words: the overheard, untaught vocabulary of other people's agonies – the deaths one was supposed to cancel out by growing as fast as possible into the War's other dreams. A choice of words to catch and be caught by; the nurturing rooms (painted spaces, the window still level with my ear, the dark, close, splinter and varnish floor) and the blank but real alternatives so near down the road – to say now that they were steel mills or bomb sites leaves so much out: the people and what they might have said or been unable to say as their choices vanished in the dust and the cold wind. My father sheltered in the cellars with his pupils as the school above was destroyed; he and the other teachers went to the children's homes after that. But he chose to have nothing to say about such events. 'Blitz', 'steel', 'rations' and 'education' are attached, for me, not to people, not to what they taught, but to what I saw, speechless, and left behind. We moved South and Sheffield became a few train journeys, childhood illnesses, parents' incomprehensible, legendary friends, a red dot on the school map of England, listed, revised and examined for an economic rôle whose textbook meanings filled in nothing like the pictures that I found growing with me and inescapable. I learned as hard as I could about the mines and heavy industry of the mindless, unlived-in North; a careless geography. But the house grew – colourless, soundless and thinner. Its surfaces stretched and tautened enough to let light through; it was under my feet holding up everything and colluding with nothing: a giant drift net, the pictures struggling and shining like the morning catch waiting to be hauled in.

> Exhausted and half-betrayed
> these irresolute landscapes
> take their places, sleepless
> furtive and alien. To be seen
> and to see with – whatever
> you can add now only makes it

more worthy of omission
or, for the sake of the dead,
at least to be known and loved
without comfort or familiarity –
a journey at night
past glowing mill windows,
a valley with a waterfall
that was 'beautiful',
the name of a pattern
in the sky with the North
Star as close and unknown
as those who leave, as if
with nothing but laughter,
their limbs stretching
like a cat's, untouchable,
in the summer grass.

Bookcase

My mother's bookcase had three shelves,
each with a lift-up, slide-in glass front,
and one wide drawer at the bottom.

As a child, I remember sitting on the floor
beside it, lifting the doors and letting them swing
and drop, at first with a satisfying bump,

and, once, with a final smash as the glass fell out.
It was order and disorder so that uniform sets
could stay together: complete Hardy (dark brown,

slim, gold-titled), Lawrence and Forster,
Mansfield short stories, a *Golden Treasury*
and a two-volume School Prize Browning (1919).

But between all these were sets of beautifully
illustrated (so I thought) books on trees
and flowers and birds. I remember one set

had a half-blown dandelion-clock
stamped on the spine, although, despite that
delicacy, they seemed heavy and even fuller

than Hardy with difficult print. The pictures,
pale, precise and tasteful were covered
by tipped-in tissue (like the portrait in the

Collected Poems of Brooke, next on the shelf).
Plant anatomy, dissected stalks and
Latin names – the proper way to see the garden

that only grown-ups knew; nature
textualised, that written graft
that out-performed the pleasures

of perception, duty bound to study.
One book that I looked through far more often
than the novels (or the *Trees*) had stills

from Kearton's films – *Nanook of the North*,
something about the Arran Islands. It was
those other people, with craggy, sunburned faces,

stuck in the sepia photo' prints, that drew me back.
It was a sort of thrilling knowledge, unbelievable
that people looked like that. In the bottom drawer

were tightly packed collections of brochures
and post-cards from 1920s Normandy. And snaps
(fading, home-developed contact-prints):

my mother and father in a rowing boat, laughing,
Chartres and Rouen, also in contact-print brown
as distant as those film-stills from my primitive world.

It was just after one war and before another
and it seems more and more important now
to understand why these pictures took their place

with the identification of birdsong and flower
patterns and trees; the shelves of things that held
together, with other countries just outside the door,

diagrams that promised complete recognition,
generous sounds that free explorers brought to book.
Still, unpossessed and, I think, encased in terror.

Great Uncle John

I never met Great Uncle John who came back from Egypt
with medals and a small cartridge pad of his own water-
colours. These were, I am sure, the first pictures I had
ever seen of that place. We inherited also a Victorian
stereo viewer and a box of double photos of the pyramids
and camels and the Sphinx with lines of native people
and well-shod, bespectacled governors. I imagine, now,
that he might have bought these polished gadgets after
his return – a different, more modern and acceptable
souvenir to give the right impression. It was in our toy-
box with tin cars and plasticine – the days before nine-
teenth century artifacts were anything but crude, out-
dated bric-a-brac to be played with and chucked. The
photos seemed right. As you held the wooden frame to
your eyes, uncomfortable and heavy on your nose like
opticians' eye-test specs and with some special antique
smell, and relaxed the muscles of your line of sight for the
first time, the two pyramids became one and settled, four
square, in the play-room space. But they were just black
and white (brown and grey), my child's eyes soon dis-
satisfied with dull old ways of seeing yet older worlds.
But the water-colours seemed alive, frightening even.
They were of water – the Nile, the Canal, lakes with palm
trees – and objects that had become pure colour, the
palest, purple-green foliage and warm earth. You could
see the grain of the hand-made paper that made each
picture deep and bright and mysterious. I remember no
deserts, no tombs, no soldiers or peasants. Not, of
course, like Scottish lochs and burns with palm-fringed
decoration, but ignoring the powers that be, it was a vision
as selective as the patent stereo perspectives. It was
personal, tangible – no static, 3D glass aquarium; the feel
of known, hand-me-down clothes. Worth a bit, now, I
suppose. The pad vanished from a removal van between
London and Leeds – impossible to prove anything and
the driver was long gone before I checked. There is a
medal left in a button-box in the attic. I think I know
where it is, or might be.

I would dip a cup in the Nile.
White China. There, a tiny floating
pool with green strings and flakes and soil
of Africa swirling in the perfect circle

in my hand. It would never settle.
It was brown against the flawless glaze.
The undrinkable water might be used for art.
I sat at dawn beside trees, the book

on my knee, and opened the box of paints
and, with my nail, flicked at the dry,
fine squirrel brush; the dust of mud
and pigments flourished, yesterday's scene

in the air. Before dipping in the cup
I slowly drew the brush against my lips;
that gentle love, those Northern creatures.
And so, enough, the first wash.

As the paper bumps and softens
the lake is really there before me.
Grass and roots settle in, share
the white texture. It's early

but I'll make it sunset – and there
the last visible clouds, livid red,
the brush, a weighty globe of water;
dilute, and dilute again, since
no-one will believe. And do I?

Baggage

A long voyage home across the sea now starts
at night with the lights and grid patterns of
New York leaping at the plane window, a
fast, steep turn, we're hardly off the ground, and
that moment when the engines slow and the

illuminated map below seems still
(are we turning back?) but, no, the black sky
takes its place all round, and as the gangways
flatten, along come the drinks, the warnings
about smoking and stringy headphones that

crackle and get in the way. Three thousand
miles compressed to a film, a dinner and
half an hour of fitful sleep. You're hardly
aware of the changed course at Bangor, Maine,
or Anticosti Island, landfall at

Shannon or the next steep turn to the east
of Manchester for a landing into
the prevailing west wind. Quite routine stuff
even if your heart jumps when the thing hits
turbulence and you're only half awake.

What I wanted to write was something to
do with a member of my family in
the last century who worked in sailing
ships, who sailed from the East, racing in his
own way home for landing slots with the wealth

of his day in tea and wool, whose name I
once saw on a list of the Cutty Sark's
crew (it could easily be someone else
though it would be nice) and who became a
captain on the Stranraer-Ireland ferry.

I wonder what became reduced, refined,
then for passengers and crew, waiting for
the wind, the currents and the tide? What he
would select to tell his tale of a calm
voyage from China or Melbourne, and what

was precious enough to be saved at all
costs or too frightening to recall for
anyone? Or, perhaps he was simply
a technician, a driver following
rules; the adrenalin rendered needless

by sticking to the almanac and sums
with dividers and a compass, as dull
as with modern Charley, Foxtrot, Romeo,
Zero language and pre-programmed fly-by-
wire ascents and landings. Perhaps he just

did it, like any other job. And for
our daughters, I wonder, too, what they will
select from the voyages home? From the
language that knows no fear? And to draw out,
after a safe landing, and the baggage

reclaimed, from things that seemed unspeakable?
You're safe. You can say it; pass it on.

Note 1: Our Photographs

I was in two minds as to whether to name the speaker of each poem. The sequence has never been conceived as a series of dramatic monologues and if there are elements of narrative there is no hidden plot. The poems do not attempt to capture any real accent or to prop themselves up with research. Some of them spring from a conscious verbal frustration, only finding themselves in a deliberate division between passages of prose and verse. I hope there is no tone of lament; it is certainly not intended that they pose as documents.

Some facts of history seemed so attention-seeking that they would immediately burst out of a poem. If facts are part of the background to these poems (for example, that Mr Gladstone sent warships and troops to the island of Skye in 1882 to quell 'riots') they are important precisely because they seem largely to have slipped out of the British memory. Moved and shocked as one might be by such rediscoveries, I can find no single voice to fill in the spaces now. One recognises that as the rifts in memory have been stretched and thinned – particularly by the physical distances of travel – certain questions concerning the subjects which just happen to be forgotten persist. But, even so, these poems can hardly claim to be answers, avoiding the obvious battles as they do.

The discovery of America, a continuing process, effected the dissolution of certain cultures and identities whilst new maps were being unrolled. Europeans watched through the confident, all-excluding lenses of Empire. And the self-evident truths of the new world did not always reach home. Broader views may have become possible in the vulnerable spaces of the West; however, in the old world, small islands proved even easier targets for colonisation and experiment and have continued to echo greater movements of history with forgettable rapidity. Islands, neatly subject to artistic imagination and political whims, were also being discovered at the same time as they were being cleared. The freedoms of landlord, pioneer or tourist betray the strangest of revisionist memories; leaving their cares behind, they leave a lot to be desired.

The facts of exploration and discovery are one thing. The records – pictures, words or photographs – are another. From the time of the earliest voyages to America artists have been taken along. Sometimes the record is 'brought back'. Sometimes it is intended to remain at the point of discovery. Whether of the 'scene' – holiday beach or desolate forest – or a new home or a family group, it celebrates and confirms both distance and identity. In the nineteenth century even those who had died in the mass migrations Westwards were photographed. Some of the grimmer roots of the poems in this sequence about America will be found in the photographs collected in *Wisconsin Death Trip* by Michael Lesy. There is no picture postcard of the Indian Well near the village of Barker, Niagara County, a few hundred yards from Lake Ontario although the local history society has written it up. The photograph referred to in the title poem is by the New York painter and photographer Nancy Shaver.

For contrast, and to see a strange inversion of the process of discovery and recording at work (the Imperial art at home), one might recall the following:

> The grandeur of the scenery was heightened by the fineness of the day, and still more by the idea that a single puff of wind might prove fatal to us, by raising the whole fury of the Western Ocean. At last came two boats, one belonging to the place and ours besides, but both manned by the *savages*. This alarmed us: we thought that our party must be lost or taken and the arms chest was instantly opened; but the boats approaching we found the natives quite pacific, and several came on board – among others their priest, without whom nothing would induce them to venture near us.

This tone did not spring from the natural perils of a voyage to the new world but it seemed natural enough to Lord Brougham in 1799 as he described St Kilda in his *Tour in the Western Isles*. The quotation is noted in Derek Cooper's *Road to the Isles* and he also records that, by the twentieth century, the St Kildans were 'laid low by cupidity: in the manner of Red Indians on reservations they even began charging to have their photographs taken'.

Be that as it may, the photographs of a doomed community have all the power and poignancy of words from a dying language. That way of seeing things cannot be repeated. I was privileged recently to see the original photographs taken by Mr Frank Lowe on St Kilda just before that community was resettled on mainland Scotland in 1930. These pictures were stored in his attic, along with the heavy plate cameras he used, in Bolton. He died in 1985, perhaps appropriately, on another expedition in Canada. The interested reader may see some of his pictures reproduced in Tom Steel's *The Life and Death of St Kilda*.

Note 2: To the Niagara Frontier

The Niagara River flows some 35 miles north from Lake Eire to Lake Ontario and it marks an area of historic conflict between British, American, French and native American people; it is still called 'The Niagara Frontier'. People could cross the relatively narrow river from the United States to Canada. They could also follow the river bank, along the Portage up the escarpment and beside the Falls, to gain access to the upper Great Lakes. There were opportunities for trade, settlement, travel and war. The Forts built on each side of the River still eye each other, oddly reflecting how European dreams of imperial power gave over a new imperial power to the New World. They are some of the earliest stone buildings in the U.S. and Canada still standing.

Even before the War of 1812 between the British and the United States over who should control the area the hinterland on both sides of the River was opened up to immigration and development. The results are today strangely complex, concentrated and visible. The sound of the Falls could be heard, it is said, up to fifteen miles away in the time of Fenimore Cooper and Dickens. Coming from water that is controlled by the Hydro-Electric plant and surrounded by industry the sound is now held to a few yards. But within the fifteen mile radius are a military airbase, the Tuscorora Indian reservation, some of the worst chemical pollution in the world, the 'Honeymoon Capital of the World' and the fruit farms of the descendants of the original settlers.

The Frontier both takes and gives; I have many reasons to be grateful. The title of this book is intended to represent a sense of direction and as a tribute.